HEAVEN HILL

written by CHERI DECKER

WestBow Press books may be ordered through booksellers or by contacting:

WestBow Press
A Division of Thomas Nelson & Zondervan
1663 Liberty Drive
Bloomington, IN 47403
www.westbowpress.com
844-714-3454

Cover and Interior Image Credit: Frida Cornelio
Interior Image Credit: Vecteezy.com

ISBN: 978-1-6642-6595-0 (sc)
ISBN: 978-1-6642-6596-7 (e)

Library of Congress Control Number: 2022908348

Print information available on the last page.

WestBow Press rev. date: 6/25/2022

WestBow
PRESS®
A DIVISION OF THOMAS NELSON
& ZONDERVAN

To Elli, who inspires others to talk with God
every day, accept His love, and take time
to enjoy God's wonderful creation.

One day a new family moved
in next door.
Mom, Dad and two children;
they numbered four.

First there was Elli with skin so fair,
sunbeams dancing in her hair.

Elli found a place where she
could talk to the Lord.

She showed her brother, Breck,
and he got on board.

The place was a mound,
so green was the grass.

They'd lay on their backs
and watch the clouds pass.

Elli declared it the best place still...

So, she claimed it and named it

HEAVEN HILL!

There was Elli and Breck
then along came Brynn.

So, Elli told her of Heaven Hill
all over again.

A place of joy with no expectation;
to worship God or quiet meditation,
where they danced before the Lord
without hesitation.

Somersaults, cartwheels, joy did abound,
whenever they played on the
Heaven Hill mound.

Sometimes they'd have a picnic,
sometimes look at the stars,

and speak with their God
who made Jupiter and Mars.

Then Landree was born and, oh,
how much fun.

It was almost like Heaven Hill
had just begun.

Finally, they had a new
brother named Crew,
and this time all the kids
knew what to do.

They took him to Heaven Hill for him to enjoy, and he became Heaven Hill's sweet baby boy!

Visitors are always welcome
on Heaven Hill if you want
to play or just sit still.
A place to rest your mind
and put it at ease,

a place to escape from
sadness or disease.
A moment in time just for resting,
and give thanks to the Lord
for every blessing.

Then the children moved away,
and Heaven Hill's chair was
empty that day.

But God is really everywhere,
no matter where you place your
blanket or your chair.

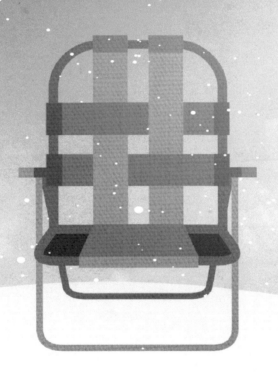

If it's too far to travel and
come all this way,
you can have Heaven Hill
in your heart today.
Regardless of the season or time of day,
Heaven Hill is always just a prayer away.
Excitement abounds for each person
who finds the secret of Heaven Hill
within their own minds.

If you are someone longing
to know God still,
accept His love into your heart
and think about Heaven Hill.
And the good things of the Lord...
you will have your fill!

You're sure to leave
Heaven Hill with a smile.

Because it's there you're reminded

You are God's Special Child !

Printed in the United States
by Baker & Taylor Publisher Services